Car Mechanic

Earning $50,000–$100,000 with a High School Diploma or Less

Earning $50,000–$100,000 with a High School Diploma or Less

Car Mechanic

Christie Marlowe

Mason Crest

Mason Crest
450 Parkway Drive, Suite D
Broomall, PA 19008
www.masoncrest.com

Printed in the United States of America.

First printing
9 8 7 6 5 4 3 2 1

Series ISBN: 978-1-4222-2886-9
ISBN: 978-1-4222-2889-0
ebook ISBN: 978-1-4222-8925-9

The Library of Congress has cataloged the
hardcopy format(s) as follows:

Library of Congress Cataloging-in-Publication Data

Marlowe, Christie.
Car mechanic / Christie Marlowe.
pages cm. – (Earning $50,000 - $100,000 with a high school diploma or less)
Includes bibliographical references and index.
ISBN 978-1-4222-2889-0 (hardcover) – ISBN 978-1-4222-8925-9 (ebook) – ISBN 978-1-4222-2886-9 (series)
1. Automobiles–Maintenance and repair–Vocational guidance–Juvenile literature. 2. Automobile mechanics–Juvenile literature. I. Title.
TL152.M2735 2014
629.28'72023–dc23

2013015554

Produced by Vestal Creative Services.
www.vestalcreative.com

Contents

CHAPTER 1

Careers Without College

One thing that most Americans could never do without is their car. It is more than just the way we get around. Whether we use it is to commute to work, go shopping, visit friends or family, or just relax, it is where we spend a substantial amount of our time. In fact, ABC News has reported that 220 million Americans spend an average of an hour and a half in their car each day!

While many people are given credit for having had a hand in inventing the modern automobile, German engineer Karl Benz, invented the first "motorwagen" in 1895. Ever since this groundbreaking invention, there has been a group of men and women who have become a necessary part of keeping America moving: car mechanics.

The motorwagen created by Karl Benz in 1895.

While Benz's invention led to the first car mechanics, the history of the mechanic actually goes much further back than the end of the nineteenth century. As long as there have been machines, there have been mechanics. Machines break, and they will do so even faster without adequate care. Mechanics are men and women with knowledge of tools, **engineering**, and **technology** who build, repair, and care for our machines.

Looking at the Words

Engineering is the branch of science focused on the design, building, and use of machines and structures.

The machines and tools developed from scientific knowledge is called **technology**.

Since the spread of the car's use in America, car mechanics have taken on a special and important role in the lives of most anyone who owns a car. They are the people we depend on not only to keep our cars on the road but also to make sure that our cars are driving dependably and safely.

By repairing and maintaining a machine that the majority of Americans depend on every day, car mechanics provide a service that many of us consider a necessity. Being a car mechanic is a difficult career that requires a number of skills in many different areas. Despite how important and skilled these men and women are, one thing that most of them do not have, however, is a college education.

The College Question

"I wouldn't change a thing," says Lindsay Valencia, summing up her ten years of experience as a car mechanic. "I really like my job. And on top

Stock car races are a great way to get excited about cars. The mechanics who work in the pit stops have to move FAST.

of that, the pay is good. Every time someone drives away from our shop with their fixed, I still feel good inside. I like knowing that I am helping people."

Lindsay began to consider whether or not she would go on for a college education while she was in high school. "Both my parents are college educated," she says, "and, they both did pretty well financially. When I was in high school, my parents and I both assumed that I would go to college too. Thing was, though, I had no idea what I wanted study. I didn't really have any big career goals at that point. In my sophomore year of high school, though, the guidance counselor at my school asked me, 'If you could do anything with a million dollars, what would it be?' At first, I came up with all the answers buy some clothes, go on a vacation, things like that. But he kept pushing me to think about long-range goals, something I would really want to do with my life if I could do anything at all. My family had always loved NASCAR"—the National Association of Stock Car Auto Racing—"so I finally said I thought maybe I would want to build racecars. I loved cars, but I had never thought about working on them. After that, though, I had this little thought in the back of my head. About a year later, I took a class on automobile repair that my high school offered. That's when I realized this could be a real job. It was something I would really love doing."

Like most young people today, Lindsay's experiences during her high school years helped shape her future. Many students, by this time, are old enough to begin to explore old hobbies or take on new ones. Both in and out of high school young people are given the opportunity to learn about themselves and the world. But even though no two young people learn and grow alike, as students prepare to graduate high school, almost all of them are asked the same question: "Is college the best choice for you?"

Do You Have a Passion?

There's a lot of talk about passion these days: "Find your passion... Pursue your passion... Do what you love..."

Passion, it turns out, lives in all sorts of places. And while finding your passion is an elusive pursuit, there is only one real formula: try things. Try things and see how they fit. Try jobs and find out what you like—and just as important, find out what you don't like.

The most important thing is: don't feel overwhelmed if you don't have a passion. Don't feel like there's something wrong with you. And then ask yourself: What is something I enjoy doing? What is something I've done already that had aspects to it I liked?

Passion can come later. Right now, just find something you enjoy. That's a starting point. Maybe it'll become that thing you can do for hours and it feels like only a few minutes have gone by. But don't put that pressure on yourself. Start small.

"Our work is to discover our work
and then with all our heart to give ourselves to it."
—Buddha

Adapted from the essay "The Truth About Finding Your Passion" by Colin Ryan. More of his work can be found at his website: http://astanduplife.com.

This is an important question and for many high school graduates today, the answer to this question is "yes." In 2011, nearly seven out of every ten students who graduated high school went on attend college.

While many people see college as the safest, if not the only way to be successful, there are many other ways a person can find a well-paying career. The United States Bureau of Labor Statistics lists over forty high-paying jobs that do not require a college education—and according to CNN, half of all college graduates are either unable find a job or ended up finding a job that didn't even require a college degree!

CNN also reported that the average student, in 2012, graduated college nearly $27,000 in debt. This much debt takes an average of 10 years to pay off! So while college may seem like the best way to land a well-paying job, considering every option is an important step before deciding what kind of career to pursue and how to acquire the skills necessary to be successful.

Learning Outside the Classroom

According to Lindsay, an education doesn't always mean sitting in a classroom—but an education does always mean that you're willing to learn. When she explains why a college education was not the right choice for her, Lindsay says, "It's not because I didn't want to learn. I always loved learning. I'm learning every day. There is so much to learn about cars. The technology these days is pretty amazing. And it keeps getting more and more complicated. So that means there is always more for me to learn. People think that cars are all the same—but actually, there are about a million tiny differences between each make and model. You could read every book on car repair there is and you'd still

There are lots of parts to learn about if you want to be a car mechanic. Here, a mechanic is cleaning a brake pad.

be surprised by how much you do not know."

Not only is learning an important part of starting a career as a car mechanic, but it is also an important part of being a successful mechanic. As the technology becomes more **intricate** and complex, so do our cars. Only recently, a mechanic's job was purely mechanical work, but now mechanics need a much broader base of knowledge. Cars have come a long ways since the earliest models back in the nineteenth century! "These days," Lindsay says, "there is always some new technology that's **revolutionizing** the industry. My boss talks about how back in the 1980s, there was a big rush to learn computer technology. Now that's just standard, because all new models since then have computers. When I was starting out, the new thing was hybrid and clean-diesel technology. I had to learn about electric cars. And they keep changing. I've had to learn two or three whole new electrical systems."

Looking at the Words

Something that is **intricate** is very detailed and complicated.

Revolutionizing means completely changing.

The automobile repair class Lindsay took her junior year of high school was a turning point for her. "I found out I loved everything about car repair. I liked getting my hands dirty, I liked working with my hands, I liked that feeling you get when you suddenly figure out what's wrong with an engine—and you can fix it! I loved it all. I was so excited, it was like falling in love!"

When Lindsay told her parents how much she enjoyed her automotive repair class they encouraged her to speak to a local mechanic, a friend of her father's who had been working on the family's cars for many years. "He let me go to the repair shop twice a week and watch

If you know someone who knows how to work on cars, ask if you can help. You'll find out if this is work you enjoy, and at the same time, you'll be getting some hands-on training to get you started.

him work," Lindsay says. "He would explain what the different parts were for, and he told me how to use some of the basic tools. He explained the clues he used to **diagnose** car problems. When business was slow, he'd let me try out some basic repairs. He was really kind and patient with me, never made me feel like I was just a stupid kid getting in his way."

Looking at the Words

To **diagnose** is to identify an illness or a problem.

A **fulfilling** job is one that is very satisfying and rewarding.

Not everyone will have the chance to develop his or her skills in the same way Lindsay did, but her story makes an important point: Lindsay spent her free time exploring her interests and learning. She took time to become passionate about something. Eventually, that passion turned into a **fulfilling** and well-paying career.

"By the time I graduated high school," Lindsay says, "I knew I didn't want to go to college. My parents weren't too surprised. They could see how happy I was working on cars, and they just kept telling me they believed in me. So that's how it all started—and it's worked out well."

CHAPTER 2

What Do Car Mechanics Do?

Car mechanics inspect, repair, and maintain cars and light trucks. Most car mechanics work either for a **dealership** where cars are sold or for an independent repair shop. Dealerships usually focus on the repair and maintenance of a specific brand of cars, Toyota or Ford for example. Independent repair shops either service all small vehicles or **specialize** in one portion of repair and maintenance, such as auto-body repair. Independent repair shops can either be large chains of repair

Looking at the Words

A **dealership** is a business that sells goods or services for a larger company.

To **specialize** is to become an expert in something.

shops or local privately owned shops.

While car mechanic duties vary depending on where they work, all car mechanics can be broken down into two categories: journeymen and master mechanics. Journeymen are responsible for general tasks, such as maintenance, and they usually specialize in the kinds of parts that they repair. Master mechanics can repair virtually every part of the vehicle. In some cases, they specialize in repairing the transmission system—a very complicated part of a car that sends power from the engine to the wheels.

Journeymen

"All master mechanics start out as journeymen," says Justin Giambruno, a master mechanic who owns his own repair shop. "To get certified as a master mechanic, you need at least two years of experience as a journeyman—and a lot of knowledge about the different systems in a car."

When Justin says "systems in a car" he is referring to the connected parts of a car that work together to make a certain portion of the car—the brakes or the air conditioner, for example—do their jobs. The Bureau of Labor Statistics lists five different types of journeymen based on the kinds of systems they repair and the duties for which they are responsible:

- **Automotive air-conditioning repairers** install and repair air conditioners and service parts. They are trained in government regulations related to their work and the kind of environmentally dangerous chemicals that are involved in a car's air conditioning system.

- **Brake repairers** adjust brakes, replace parts of the brakes that wear down over time, and make other repairs on brake systems. Some technicians specialize in both brake and front-end work.
- **Front-end mechanics** align and balance wheels and repair steering mechanisms and suspension systems. They frequently use special alignment equipment and wheel-balancing machines.
- **Transmission technicians and rebuilders** work on gear trains, couplings, hydraulic pumps, and other parts of transmissions. Extensive knowledge of computer controls, the ability to diagnose electrical and hydraulic problems, and other specialized skills are needed to work on these complex components.
- **Tune-up technicians** adjust or replace parts to ensure that the engine is running efficiently. They often use electronic testing equipment to find and fix problems in fuel, ignition, and emissions control systems.

According to Justin, when a journeyman works on only one of these areas, he is called a "specialty technician"; however, it is very rare to find any journeyman that works on only one of these systems. "Most repair shops will have one or two master mechanics working for them. At my shop, the master mechanic owns the business. That's pretty common. But all repair shops have journeymen to take care of the small jobs, stuff like **maintenance** and helping out with bigger jobs."

Looking at the Words

The process of keeping something in good condition is called **maintenance**.

Armando Fragomeni, center, is telling how he started out sweeping the floors in a garage, and then went on to test drive Ferraris, Lamborghinis, Mercedes, and Maseratis. Next, he became a journeyman, and ended up as a master mechanic.

Maintenances are much easier to carry out than a repair. That's because if he's doing maintenance, a mechanic doesn't need to diagnose what made something go wrong. Also, fewer parts are involved. Most car companies or "automakers" design certain parts such as air and oil filters to be maintained regularly. After a specific number of miles, all cars require certain maintenance, such as replacing the various fluids or rotating the car's tires—alternating where each tire is mounted so that each tire doesn't wear down as quickly—in order to prevent worse problems or even accidents while driving.

Other forms of maintenance occur less regularly but are still common. Parts such as brakes, batteries, and tires are not designed to last the life of a car, so they will need to be replaced at some point. Exactly when these parts will need to be replaced depends on how a person drives and how she takes care of her car. By taking care of routine maintenances, journeymen learn all the different systems of a car, what purposes they serve, and how these different systems work together. They get valuable experience that will help them get better at their career.

> **Looking at the Words**
>
> **Emissions** are the particles of pollution given off by things like cars and factories.

"Another kind of maintenance," says Justin, "is a factory recall." A factory recall happens when the car company discovers that a part installed on a specific kind of car is breaking often or is a possible safety risk. In either case, the company that made the cars begins a "recall," which means that the company either recommends or requires that an owner of the car replace the part. "Only mechanics working for car dealerships have to worry about recalls," Justin continues. "I started out working as a technician's helper in a Honda dealership, so that's why I know about recalls. Some of them were a nightmare." According to Justin, any work during a recall is free for the customer—but for journeymen it can mean replacing the same part hundreds or thousands of times in just a few weeks!

While independent repair shops don't see any recalls, they see a lot more inspections than the dealerships do. In most American states, a mechanic with a good amount of experience and a special certification from the government is required to check or "inspect" every vehicle registered in the state for safety or **emissions** problems. "When you're doing a safety check," Justin says, "you make sure the tires are in good shape. The brakes work. The lights, the horn, the windshield wipers, everything—it all has to be working. You also have to make sure the car complies to all the standards that have been set for that make." When

A journeyman will learn how to remove and replace transmissions.

a journeyman inspects the emissions of a car, she has to measure the amount of certain chemicals produced by the car when it is running. These chemicals could be harmful to the environment or to people's health. A journeyman has to hook up the car to a computer in order to analyze the amount of chemicals that the car is producing.

Master Mechanics

Master mechanic can also complete maintenance, recalls, and inspections, but journeymen usually handle these kinds of simple and routine work. Master mechanics are more likely to diagnose and handle repairs.

"Repairs," says Justin, "can be tough. It's hard to figure out what's wrong sometimes." In some cases, according to Justin, large repair shops will hire a journeyman specifically trained in diagnosing car problems, but most repair shops are not big enough for this kind of position.

"This," Justin says, "is where the master mechanics come in. When someone has years of experience, they get really good at the job. Guys like that know what to look for. They've seen it all a million times, so they know what to check." Once a diagnosis has been determined, the car can be repaired. In most cases, a journeyman with the right knowledge will actually complete the repair, but the master mechanic will tell her what to do. If the journeyman isn't very experienced with a specific system, the master mechanic will help with the repair. That way, the journeyman can continue to learn and be able to complete similar repairs in the future.

A big part of diagnosing a car problem is talking to customers, finding out how the problem started, and what were the signs that showed that the car needed to be repaired. What noises did the car make? When did it happen? What else was the car doing (for example, going fast,

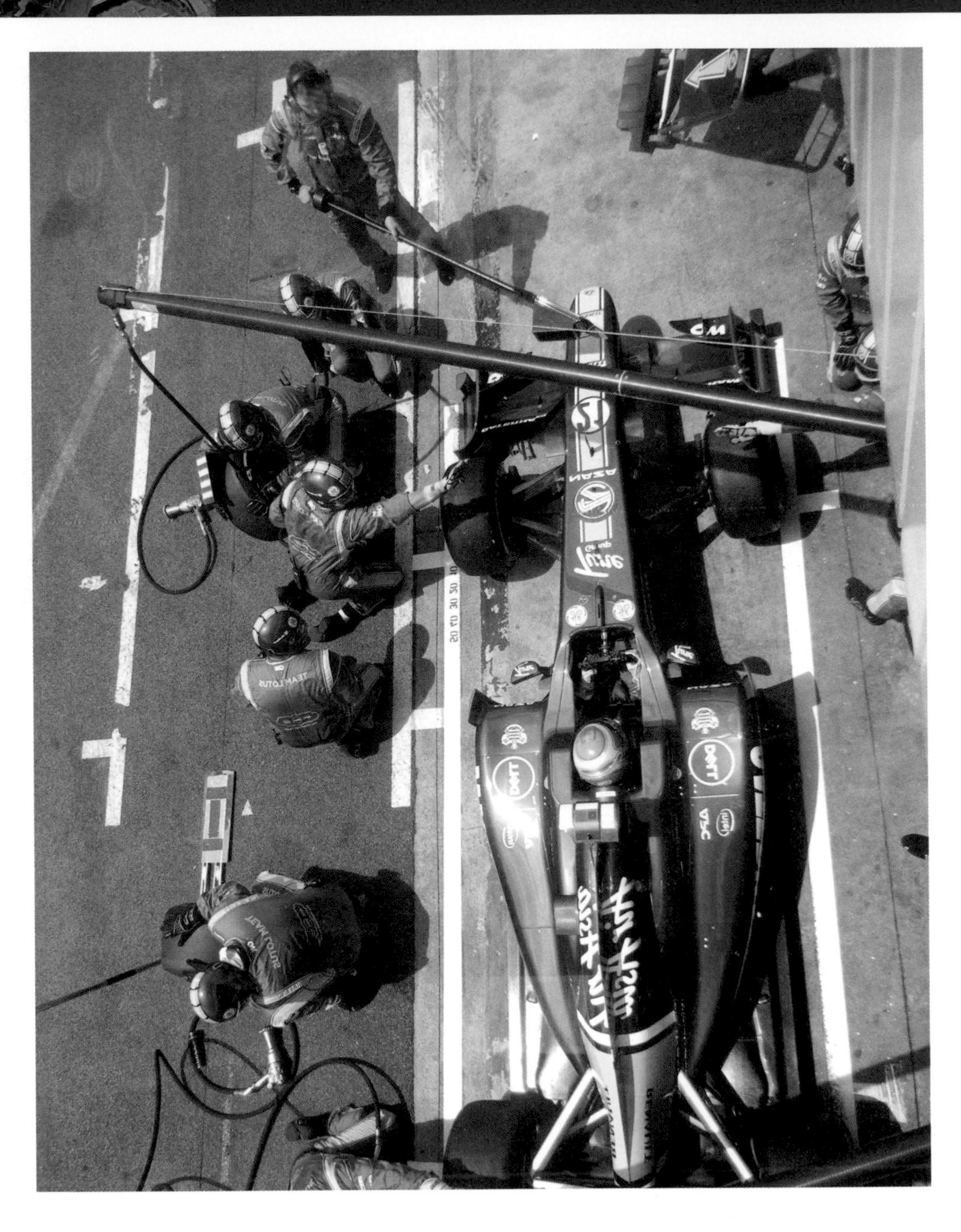

Mechanics who work on pit crews for race cars have one of the most exciting and highest-paid jobs in this field.

Take a Pit Stop

In automobile racing, a pit stop is when a racing vehicle stops during a race for refueling, new tires, repairs, mechanical adjustments, or any combination of these. Pit stop work is carried out by anywhere from five to twenty mechanics (also called a pit crew).

A pit crew in professional racing generally has nine assigned roles. A crew chief and a car chief are in charge of the pit crew before, during, and after a race is done. Seven other mechanics are responsible for working on the car when it pulls into the pit lane. Five mechanics work on changing the tires as quickly as possible, while another mechanic refuels the car. The last role of the pit crew, known as the "seventh man," is responsible for taking care of the driver's needs.

Being in a pit crew is the most exciting and by far the most dangerous job that car mechanics can get. But with this fast pace comes a great salary of at least $75,000 a year, along with a certain portion of the money that the team wins by winning the race—a portion that can equal up to $150,000 for one race!

braking, idling)? Talking to customers professionally and courteously is important, especially for diagnosing a repair.

Master mechanics usually need to customers about a lot of things. They're the ones who usually communicate to customers what work was performed to fix a car and how to prevent a repair in the future. "Talking to customers," Justin says, "is a skill you have to have if you want

An auto body mechanic is using a slide hammer to straighten a damaged fender

to be a master mechanic. People who like their mechanic turn into loyal customers. They keep coming back. Some of my customers have been coming to me for years now."

CHAPTER 3

How Can I Become a Car Mechanic?

"This is a great time to become a mechanic," says Rachel Borofsky, a newly trained journeyman who recently landed her first job as a car mechanic. "When my folks were growing up, kids—boys, especially—started working on cars when they were teenagers. Most men knew how to take care of their own cars. They didn't need a mechanic for the routine stuff. Nowadays, it's a lot more complicated. Kids are more interested in computers than

In today's world, older men are often the ones who know their way around the underside of a car. Ask around and find someone who would be willing to teach you what he knows.

cars, I think. Anyway, a lot of people would rather not touch anything under the hood of their car. Fine by me! That's why I have a job."

According to Rachel, the fact that young people are losing interest in their cars is one of the reasons why there is a shortage of car mechanics right now. Another reason is that more and more people own cars now—and as more people own cars, more cars will need to be repaired. A shortage of car mechanics means there are plenty of new jobs available for mechanics.

Is Repairing Automobiles Right for Me?

"Not everyone likes working on cars," says Rachel. "It's hard work. You have to know your way around a set of tools. You have to be willing to get dirty. Sometimes you have to lie on your back under a car for a long time." Being a car mechanic is a very "hands-on kind of job," Rachel says and a lot of people don't like working this way. "It's to like showing up to an office every day. I get that. But for me, it's a whole lot more interesting. It's tiring, yeah, but it's also like solving puzzles every day. I'm putting something together, you know what I mean? And it's a cool job, really, because pretty much anyone can learn to do it."

According to Rachel, one of the most important questions that an interested young person can ask herself is: "Is repairing automobiles right for me?"

She goes on: "Starting out as a journeyman is pretty easy. Somebody tells me what to do and when to do it. I don't have to take care of diagnosing problems. I don't have to figure out the best way to fix something. I help out with larger repairs but I'm not really responsible for the job. My job right now is to just show up, pay attention, and learn.

I figure that's the only way I'm going to make more money one day. If you want to be a master mechanic, you have to be willing to work even hard. You have to like a challenge too."

Rachel doesn't plan on staying a journeyman more than the two years of experience required to take the tests to become a master mechanic. "I am not sure that two years will be enough," she says. "People tell me you really need at least three years, and some people say you should plan on taking seven years before you take the test. But I'm impatient, I guess. I love it when I have a chance to figure something out."

Rachel's advice: Examine your strengths. "The best mechanics love working with machines," she says, "and they're good at solving problems. And you have to love a challenge." If you do too, then a career as a car mechanic might be the right one for you.

What All Car Mechanics Need

While a passion for machine work and problem solving might get someone started as a good **candidate** for a career as a car mechanic, a car mechanic should have certain other skills as well. The Bureau of Labor Statistics lists six important qualities that every car mechanic should have.

- **Customer-service skills**. Mechanics must discuss automotive problems—along with options for fixing them—with their customers. Because self-employed workers depend on repeat clients for business, they must be courteous, good listeners, and ready to answer customers' questions.

- **Detail oriented**. Mechanical and electronic malfunctions are often due to misalignments or other easy-to-miss reasons. Service mechanics must, therefore, account for such details when inspecting or repairing engines and components.
- **Dexterity**. Many tasks that journeymen do, such as taking apart engine parts, connecting or attaching components, and using hand tools, require a steady hand and good hand–eye coordination.
- **Mechanical skills**. Mechanics must be familiar with engine components and systems and know how they interact with each other. They must often take apart major parts for repairs and be able to put them back together properly.
- **Technical skills.** Mechanics use **sophisticated** diagnostic equipment on engines, systems, and components. They must be familiar with electronic control systems and the appropriate tools needed to fix and maintain them.
- **Troubleshooting skills**. Mechanics must be able to identify and fix problems in increasingly complicated mechanical and electronic systems.

Looking at the Words

Someone who is a **candidate** is likely to get a certain position or experience.

A machine or technology that is **sophisticated** is very complex and detailed.

Diverse means having a wide variety.

Car mechanics need a **diverse** set of skills in order to be successful, but there is one more skill that, according to Rachel, is just as

It takes intelligence, experience, and patience to diagnose problems under the hood of a car.

important as any of these skills. "Any good mechanic," Rachel says, "needs patience. I watch the guys that are really good at this. They can **troubleshoot** just about anything without getting frustrated or angry. I really respect them. Customers aren't always nice either—but my boss never loses his cool. He's always respectful, even when they're yelling at him. He has this knack for calming people down."

Practicing patience in your everyday life is one good way to prepare for being a mechanic. There are also a number of other skills you can begin to practice, no matter what field you end up with. All careers need workers who are **dependable** and **responsible**. People need to know they can count on you. Every employer also enjoys a positive attitude, because positive people will not be discouraged by a challenge. And since for most **entry-level** positions you'll work under the supervision of one or many people more experienced than you are, you also need to be able to work as a team and to take directions.

Looking at the Words

To **troubleshoot** is to solve problems with a machine.

If you are **dependable**, you are reliable and trustworthy.

A person who is **responsible** does what she says she will do.

An **entry-level** job is one that requires only basic skills and will lead to more jobs later on.

If you already have some of these skills, you are already well on your way to an exciting career as a car mechanic. If you are not very strong in some of these areas, then now is the time to begin to learn and explore.

Becoming a Car Mechanic

There are also many practical skills a person needs in order to begin a career in this field. Many of these skills will be learned on the job. "But," Rachel says, "the best way to begin a career as a mechanic is to start working on cars as young as you can. The more you can learn on your own or from hanging out with people who are already good

You can also learn how to be a car mechanic in the military. This auto skills center is part of the U.S. Marines' Camp Pendleton.

mechanics, the better off you'll be. After that, you might want to get an **apprenticeship** or go to a **vocational** school."

According to Rachel, if you're interested in becoming a car mechanic, there are things you can do while you're still a teenager. "All mechanics have to have a high school degree or a **GED**," Rachel says. "You can't just blow off school because you've decided not to go to college." Mechanics need reading skills for studying **manuals** to learn how to repair specific problems or replace certain parts. You may also use math, and you'll definitely have to work with computers. Most high schools have computer classes, which will help get you ready to work with the electrical systems of cars as well as the computers used to diagnose problems.

Looking at the Words

An **apprenticeship** is a training program for people learning how to do a job.

Something that relates to employment is **vocational**.

GED stands for General Equivalency Degree. It is a substitute for a high school diploma, for those who did not finish high school.

Manuals are books of instruction.

Some high schools have automotive repair classes that teach a young person some simple automotive basics under the supervision of a professional. "No one," Rachel says, "wants to just open the hood of a car and start playing around. If you don't know what you are doing, you could hurt the car—or yourself." Some communities now have technical high schools where young people learn machine work while taking the classes required for a high school diploma. Programs like AYES (Automotive Youth Educations Systems) provide educational classes and resources to high schools or groups of interested young people.

Vocational school—also known as a technical school—is another great alternative to college for people interested in becoming mechanics. Vocational schools offer training in a specific set of skills for a specific industry. These programs are much shorter than college, generally between six months and two years, and they are much cheaper than

Some repair shops like this one will hire apprentices. This means you will get paid while you are trained to be a mechanic.

college. "My technical school," says Rachel, "lasted a little less than a year—and it only cost me a few thousand dollars. I worked as a waitress to pay for it. When I finished, the school helped me find me the job that I have now. I finished free of debt. And I have a great job."

Though these are less and less common, especially in certain areas, another way to enter the automotive field is to get an apprenticeship. Automotive apprentices may have very little experience in car mechanics, but a repair shop hires them in order to teach them what they need to know on the job. Apprenticeships are usually longer than a vocational school—about four years—and they sometimes involve classes at community colleges in engineering and advanced automotive repair.

No matter how you get the skills that you need, the small investment of time and money compared to a college education means that pretty much anyone can be qualified for an exciting career as a car mechanic.

CHAPTER 4

How Much Can I Make?

How much a car mechanic makes depends on how much training or experience she has, where she lives, and how many different kinds of repair and maintenance work she knows how to handle. For someone who becomes a mechanic through an apprenticeship or a vocational school, how much he is paid depends, in part, on how well and how quickly he can learn to work with all of the different systems in a car.

A master mechanic will need to know how to repair a torque transmission like this one.

High-Level Earnings

"If you want to earn a big salary," says Alex McRaniels, "you have to learn fast, work fast, and get certified." Alex has been a master mechanic for over ten years. He lives and works in Alaska, the state where mechanics are paid the most on average. When he says "get certified," he means becoming certified as a technician experienced and capable of repair and maintenance of different automobile systems. Getting certified in all the systems in light cars and trucks means that you have been awarded the status of a master mechanic.

You need to pass eight tests in order to become a master mechanic, but you cannot take any of these tests without at least two years of experience as a journeyman. These tests, given by a group called the ASE (the National Institute of Automotive Service Excellence), are to prove your knowledge and ability to repair these aspects of a car: engines, automatic transmissions, **manual drive trains**, **suspension** and steering systems, brakes, electrical systems, heating and air conditioning, and engine performance.

"Once you have passed all of the ASE tests," Alex says, "you have to get recertified every five years. The recertification tests aren't as long as when you take them the first time. But you can't afford to get too rusty in an area. If you do, you could lose your master status." In other words, a mechanic can never stop learning! But certification as a master

Looking at the Words

Manual drive trains are the systems that move the energy from an engine to the wheels of a car.

On a car, the **suspension** is the system that keeps the car cushioned from getting bounced around on the road.

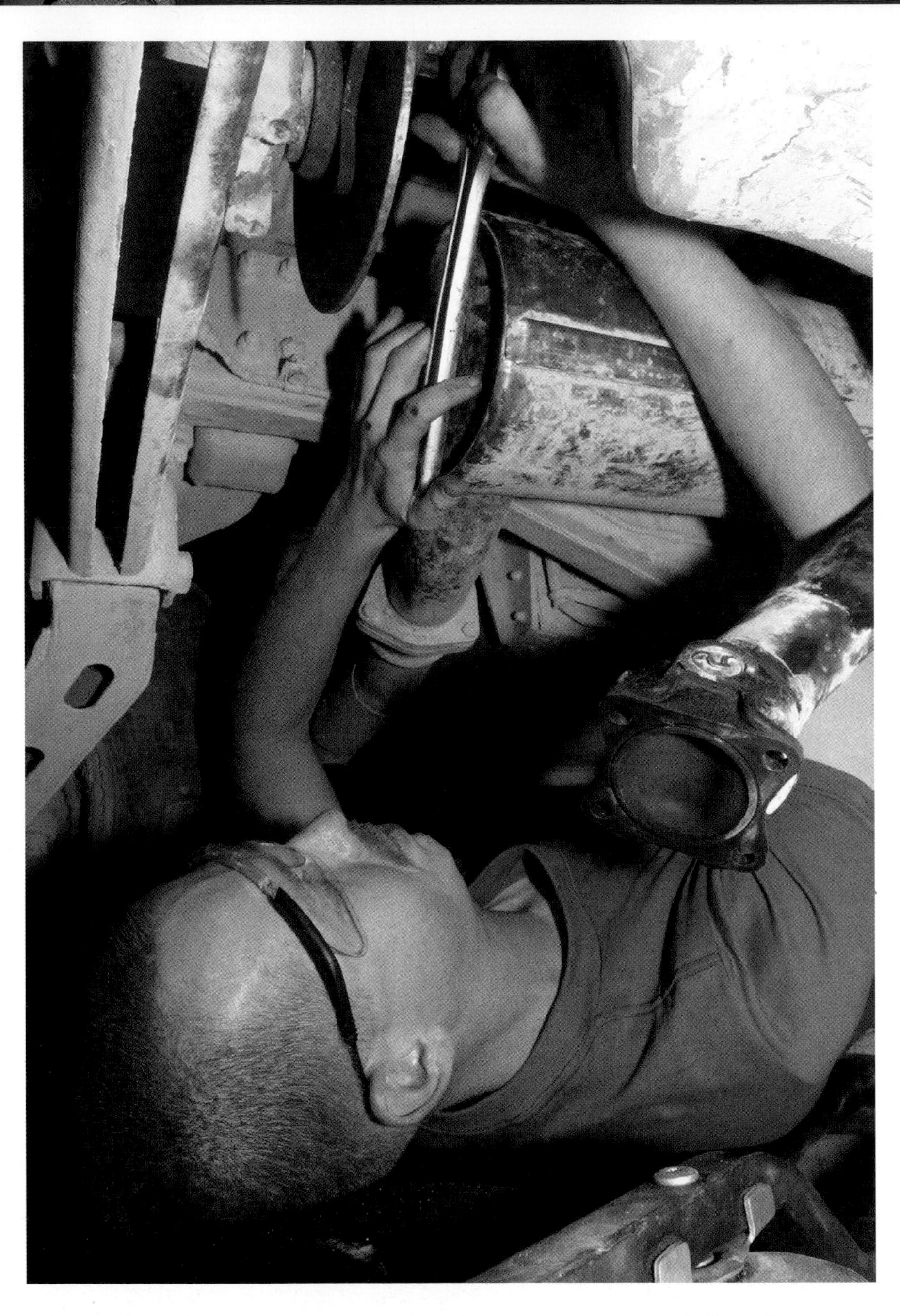

Master mechanics may oversee journeymen while they do work such as replacing drive shafts.

mechanic gives you access to better job opportunities and higher wage. You will be able to oversee other mechanics and technicians under you. Some master mechanics, like Justin from chapter 2, choose to open their own shops, which may allow them to make more money.

Master mechanics who own their own shops certainly make the most money of all mechanics, but they also function as business owners. This means they have many responsibilities outside of maintaining and repairing cars. Depending on the size of the shop, almost all master mechanics will hire other master mechanics and journeymen to do much of car work for them.

Alex, on the other hand, decided not to open up his own shop. He enjoys his career as a master mechanic. "I make great money," he says. "I don't see why I would want to worry myself with owning a business."

Like most highly skilled and highly experienced car mechanics, Alex makes a certain portion of the money that the customer is charged for labor, also called a "commission." This means that the more he works, the more money he makes. He is working for a Ford dealership—and he makes $61,000 dollars a year, which means, according to the Bureau of Labor Statistics, that he is a part of the 10 percent of all mechanics who earn more than $59,000 dollars a year.

Average Salaries

Salaries like Alex's are possible for any mechanic who is willing to become experienced, get certified, and take on the responsibilities of working at the head of a team of mechanics. But Alex makes an exceptionally high salary for a car mechanic who has not opened his own business.

The average car mechanic makes almost $36,000 dollars a year. But, says Alex, "When you consider all of the guys who don't get certified,

This model engine is a good place to learn. But the real-life engines you'll be working on as a car mechanic are likely to be a lot dirtier!

stay stuck as journeymen, and don't challenge themselves to work harder or learn more, that number could probably be a lot higher." Alex was already making about $39,000 a year only three years after taking his first job.

According to Alex, repairing and maintaining cars and light vehicles is a rewarding career, but it is also challenging. For some people, no amount of money would be enough to compensate them for working with machines every day. But for the men and women who have the kind of determined, problem-solving personality that being a mechanic requires, the pay is just a small bonus for the fulfillment that they get from this work. Repairing and maintaining automobiles is a fantastic and well-paying option for anyone who enjoys this kind of work.

XEBRA
ELECTRIC

CHAPTER 5

Looking to the Future

The skills required for automotive repair and maintenance are changing quickly. Mechanics only twenty-five years ago would have a very different set of skills and knowledge than most mechanics today. The future of automotive industry is in highly technical and computerized cars that will need highly skilled mechanics to repair and maintain them. But while car mechanics will need a greater base of skills and knowledge to continue to be successful and advance in their careers, one thing they still won't need is a college education.

New Technologies, New Skills

"Today," says Jada Edwards, an automotive engineer who designs engine components for a car manufacturer, "your car can have as many as fifty microprocessors"—small computers—"controlling everything from emissions to safety."

Emissions—the amount of environmentally harmful chemicals produced by a car—have been a large reason that car manufacturers today have made computers a standard part of every car they produce. As governments have started making regulations controlling the amount of emissions a car can produce, microprocessors have become standard; one of the best ways to reduce the amount of emissions produced by an engine is by carefully controlling the amount of air that is available when fuel is used by the car. Controlling this takes very precise measurements that only a computer would be able to make.

Other examples of new technologies that are drastically changing the skill set needed by our mechanics today are **hybrid** and electric cars. Hybrid cars use a combination of gas and electricity in order to greatly improve a car's miles-per-gallon—the amount of miles a car can drive for every gallon of gasoline that it uses. This means that a car's engine system and electric system need to work together in order to make the car move, and making these two systems **compatible** can be a large job for modern mechanics.

Looking at the Words

A **hybrid** car is one that is fueled by both gas and electricity.

Two things that are **compatible** work well together.

Electric vehicles, on the other hand, are at the front of the advance in automotive technology that has turned a mechanic's job from mostly mechanical work into mostly electrical and computer work. "The mechanics of the future," says Jada, "will have knowledge less like a mechanical engineer and more like an electrician or computer scientist." This trend means that mechanics are learning whole new skill sets, but it also means that exciting new technologies will be available in our cars.

"Currently," says Jada, "there are a lot of amazing new technologies being researched, which will make your car ride significantly safer and make your drive more pleasant and even fun." For example, Jada's company is currently researching an electronic sun visor that will dim the windshield of a car, depending on the direction and strength of the sun's

In order to keep up with the changing technology, today's mechanics have to work hard, work fast—and learn fast too.

rays. Her company is also working on a system of cameras that will be able to tell if a driver has fallen asleep at the wheel, wake him up, and keep him from getting into an accident. According to Jada, though her company isn't working on it, the German government is even researching a project that will use a system of cameras, both in cars and on the road, that will take care of most traffic jams!

Driving with Your Brain

The Discovery Channel News reported that researchers at Freie Universitat Berlin, a German university, are working on a device that will allow a driver to drive a car with her mind. The device is called BrainDriver and involves a driver taking courses beforehand to learn how to tell the computer to turn right rather than left, for example. While BrainDriver has been completed and is currently being tested, we won't see this particular application in any new cars for at least a few years. But imagine all the new skills a mechanic will have learned by the time a customer comes in to complain that his BrainDriver isn't working and he has to use his steering wheel instead!

These new technologies are not too far away. Someone interested in becoming a car mechanic should stay aware of all of the new technology that is being researched and installed in our cars today. It may very well be the technology future mechanics will have to handle on a regular basis!

A Growing Field, A Shrinking Number of Mechanics

According to the Bureau of Labor Statistics, employment for automotive service technicians and mechanics is expected to rise by 17 percent from 2010 to 2020, slightly faster than the average for all other jobs, even those that require a college degree. For anyone who gets an apprenticeship as a car mechanic or goes through some sort of vocational or technical school, getting a job will be very easy over the next few years because of a shortage in the number of mechanics who are skilled enough to work on all these new technologies.

According to Jada, the amount of new technology in a car, especially microprocessors, has been part of the reason behind the current shortage of car mechanics. "These computers keep curious people from checking under their hood. You now need another specialized computer to hook up to your car in order to tell whether or not it needs to be repaired. For a trained technician, these specialized computers make it easier to diagnose most problems with your car, especially smaller problems, which are notorious for disappearing as soon as you bring the car in for repairs. But they don't encourage the average Joe—or Jane—to start poking around under the hood." Ironically, while computers have made diagnosing car problems easier for mechanics, they have also discouraged curious young people from entering the mechanics profession. "Even though," Jada says "diagnosing problems has become easier, actually fixing the problems can be much harder unless you are specially trained

Mechanics today are learning new skills. They need to understand computerized technology, and they must be prepared to work with electric and hybrid cars. But one thing isn't going to change—if you want to be a mechanic, you have to be willing to get your hands dirty!

for these kinds of computers, especially some of the more advanced ones that are coming out today."

Part of the shortage of mechanics is because of all of the additional training that is needed for working on these complex vehicles. Automotive repair and maintenance is quickly turning into a field for highly skilled labor, which means that mechanics both now and in the future will need, above all else, to continue to learn. "But," Jada says, "A lot of this learning still happens on the job. The sooner you get into the automotive work force, the better prepared you will be once the technology changes!"

Conclusion

While the technology in our automobiles continues to grow, change, become more complex, and, as a result, make the job of a car mechanic more challenging, it is also one of the reasons that being a car mechanic today is so exciting!

Repairing and maintaining most cars manufactured today requires a very interesting mix of skills—both the ability to work with traditional machines and the knowledge of digital information technologies and computers. While many careers are available for someone who wants to work with machines (machinists, engineers, electricians) or computers (web designers, information technology specialists, software programmers), very few careers offer the change to work with both.

The people interviewed in this book are intelligent and passionate. They are working in a career that is quickly changing, which means they are constantly working to stay abreast with the latest technology. They decided that college wasn't the right choice for them not because they are unintelligent or lack ambition. Instead, they took another path to get what they wanted: a good salary, the chance to advance, and fulfilling work.

Wise Words

*"To accomplish great things we must not only act,
but also dream; not only plan, but also believe."*
Anatole France

*"Happiness is not in the mere possession of money;
it lies in the joy of achievement, in the thrill of creative effort."*
Franklin D. Roosevelt

*"Commit yourself to your own success
and follow the steps required to achieve it."*
Steve Maraboli

*"Trust yourself. Follow your interests.
They will be good guides on the path of life.
Believe in your ability to follow them
with strength and purpose."*
Anne Constance

Just maybe, if you pursue a career as a car mechanic, you'll find yourself repairing solar cars like this one day in the future!

For many people, college is the perfect choice and an important learning experience. Not only can it open the doors of certain careers, but it is also often the first experience that many young people have at living away from home, without the safety and security of their parents. College is undoubtedly a wonderful learning opportunity.

Unfortunately, many students go to college with no idea of what they want to do with their lives. In some cases, young people feel pressured by their peers or their parents into going to college without any idea where to go from there. Many students leave college still with no idea of what they want from a career. And because of the staggering debt that many students have to acquire just to go to college, they may be in a far worse financial position than they were before.

Some people go to college simply because they think they'll make more money when they get out and get a job. Even if that proves to be true, however, what good is a career if you do not enjoy doing it? Money is important—but if you're going to do something five days a week for the next forty years or so of your life, it's also important to truly like what you do.

How do you define success? There is no right answer. Answer honestly, and you will already be on your way to making the best decision for your future.

Going to college may be the best option for you. Or another road might be your road to success. Either way, consider every option and be open to all possibilities. Be willing to learn and work hard, no matter where life takes you!

Find Out More

In Books

Weintraub, Aileen. *Auto Mechanic*. Danbury, Conn.: Children's Press, 2004.

Thomas, William Davis. *Auto-Mechanics (Neighborhood Helpers)*. North Mankato, Minn.: Child's World, 2006.

Hammond, Richard. *Car Science*. New York. DK Children, 2008.

On the Internet

Automotive Youth Educational Systems
www.ayes.org

National Automotive Technicians Education Foundation
www.natef.org

National Institute for Automotive Service Excellence
www.ase.com

Bibliography

eHow.com. "What Do Car Mechanics Do?" http://www.ehow.com/about_5182587_do-car-mechanics-do_.html (accessed March 5, 2013).

Nice, Karim. "How Car Computers Work." How Stuff Works. http://auto.howstuffworks.com/under-the-hood/trends-innovations/car-computer.htm (accessed March 6, 2013).

ONeT Online. "Automotive Service Technicians and Mechanics" http://www.onetonline.org/link/summary/49-3023.00 (accessed March 3, 2013).

Teeghman, David. "The Car Your Brain Can Drive." *Discovery News*. http://news.discovery.com/tech/the-car-your-brain-can-drive.htm (accessed March 7, 2013).

U.S. Bureau of Labor Statistics. "Automotive Service Technicians and Mechanics" http://www.bls.gov/ooh/installation-maintenance-and-repair/automotive-service-technicians-and-mechanics.htm (accessed March 4, 2013).

Weisler, Paul. "6 New Car Technologies in Your Not-So-Distant Future." *Popular Mechanics*. http://www.popularmechanics.com/cars/news/4219496 (accessed March 7, 2013).

Index

About the Author

Christie Marlowe lives in Binghamton, New York, where she works as a writer and web designer. She has a degree in literature, cares strongly about the environment, and spends three or more nights a week wailing on her Telecaster.

Picture Credits

p. 6: Piotrus; p. 8: Zenodot; p. 10: U.S. Army; p. 14: AMM12; p. 16: T. Voekler; pp. 18, 22, 24: U.S. Marines; p. 26: Dell, Inc.; pp. 28, 30, 32: U.S. Marines; p. 36: Christopher Ziemnowicz; p. 38: U.S. Marines; p. 40: ANT Berezhnyi; p. 42: Mauricio Jordan De Souza Coelho | Dreamstime.com; p. 44: Petr S; p. 46: U.S. Marines; p. 48: Amal; p. 52: Infrogmation of New Orleans; p. 53: Moulessha; p. 56: Jorge Royan; p. 59: Hideki Kimara, Kouhei Sagawa